A Cry from Heaven

Vincent Woods was born in Co. Leitrim in 1960. His plays include *At the Black Pig's Dyke* (Druid Theatre Company, Druid Lane Theatre, Galway, 1992); *Song of the Yellow Bittern* (Druid Theatre Company, Druid Lane Theatre, 1994), and *On the Way Out* (Skehana Theatre Company, Glens Centre, Manorhamilton, 2002). His work has been staged in Ireland, the US, England, Canada and Australia and has been translated into French, German and Irish. He worked as a journalist and broadcaster before becoming a full-time writer. He adapted Ignazio Silone's novel *Fontamara* for stage and has written a version of Alfred Jarry's *Ubu Roi*. Two plays for children are *The Brown Man* and *The Donkey Prince*. Radio plays are *The Leitrim Hotel* and *The Gospels of Aughamore*.

He is a member of Aosdána and lives in Dublin.

T0262423

Vincent Woods

A Cry from Heaven

B L O O M S B U R Y

LONDON • NEW DELHI • NEW YORK • SYDNEY

Bloomsbury Methuen Drama

An imprint of Bloomsbury Publishing Plc

50 Bedford Square	1385 Broadway
London	New York
WC1B 3DP	NY 10018
UK	USA

www.bloomsbury.com

Bloomsbury is a registered trade mark of Bloomsbury Publishing Plc

First published 2005 by Methuen Publishing Ltd

© Vincent Woods, 2005

Vincent Woods has asserted his right under the Copyright, Designs and
Patents Act, 1988, to be identified as author of this work.

All rights reserved. No part of this publication may be reproduced or transmitted
in any form or by any means, electronic or mechanical, including photocopying,
recording, or any information storage or retrieval system, without prior permission in
writing from the publishers.

No responsibility for loss caused to any individual or organization acting on or
refraining from action as a result of the material in this publication
can be accepted by Bloomsbury or the author.

All rights whatsoever in this play are strictly reserved and application for performance
etc. should be made before rehearsals by professionals and by amateurs to Vincent Woods,
26 Primrose Street, Broadstone, Dublin 7, Ireland. Mail to: vwoods@eircom.net. No
performance may be given unless a licence has been obtained.

No rights in incidental music or songs contained in the work are hereby granted and
performance rights for any performance/presentation whatsoever must be
obtained from the respective copyright owners.

Visit www.bloomsbury.com to find out more about our authors and their books
You will find extracts, author interviews, author events and you can sign up for
newsletters to be the first to hear about our latest releases and special offers.

British Library Cataloguing-in-Publication Data
A catalogue record for this book is available from the British Library.

ISBN: PB: 978-0-4137-7539-9
          EPDF: 978-1-4081-5030-6
          EPUB: 978-1-4081-5029-0

Library of Congress Cataloging-in-Publication Data
A catalog record for this book is available from the Library of Congress.

A Cry from Heaven was first presented at the Abbey Theatre, Dublin, on 9 June 2005. The cast was as follows:

Conor	Ciaran Taylor
Ness	Olwen Fouéré
Fergus	Denis Conway
Deirdre	Kelly Campbell
Leabharcham	Gabriel Reidy
Cathach	Barry McGovern
Naoise	Alan Turkington
Ainle /Ensemble	Peter Gaynor
Ardan /Ensemble	Aidan Turner
Felim	Bosco Hogan
Black Bull /Ensemble	Charlie Kranz
White Bull /Ensemble	Tony McKenna
Red Branch Knight	Shane Gately

Director and Lighting Designer	Olivier Py
Set, Costume and Make-up Designer	Pierre-Andre Weitz
Lighting Assistant	Bertrand Killy
Stage Director	John Stapleton
Assistant Stage Managers	Stephen Dempsey
	Liz Gerhardy
Voice Director	Andrea Ainsworth
Dramaturg	Jocelyn Clarke
Assistant to the Director (Intern)	Gary Keegan

May the past be past and buried,
Made fertile ground for future peace.
May you gather a wise harvest for us all.

Fergus
Five years ago I left this court.
My choice to leave was hard –
You all know that.
I believe that I was fair as King,
Maybe not as 'wise' as might have been,
But human-hearted in my weakness.
Maybe too proud for my own good;
We'll not rehearse it all again:

My brother dies;
I ask his widow, Ness, to be my wife.
What greater honour can I show?
With one condition she accepts:
That Conor, her loved son, should reign
As King of Ulster for a year.
I thought it not too dear a price to pay:
My nephew, now my son, shown favour,
The throne his for one twelve months,
Then mine again.

All here know two years go by,
And clear as day my choice:
Stand down for good – or fight –
My brother's son, my wife . . .
No choice but leave, go into exile.

Five years in Connaught:
I could have plotted vengeance,
Raised an army to unseat this King –
They'd not be slow to march on Ulster;
But I swallowed pride and passion,
Let patience rule the day.
I did this for the sake of peace.

And now the summons to return:
Old Ulster, which grew restless at my fate

A Cry from Heaven

Characters

Conor, *King of Ulster*
Ness, *Conor's mother*
Fergus, *formerly King, Ness's husband, Conor's uncle*
Deirdre
Child Deirdre
Leabharcham, *companion to Deirdre*
Cathach, *her husband, Conor's seer*
Naoise, *Deirdre's lover, Conor's nephew*
Ainle *and* **Ardan**, *his twin brothers, Conor's nephews*
Felim, *Deirdre's father*
Deirdre's Mother
Red Branch Soldiers

Act One

Scene One

Darkness. Light like candle flames begin to glow, slowly illuminating the great feasting hall at Eamhain Macha on the night of Samhain. Other rooms stretching off. Sense of vast space, tension, power. **Ness** *and* **Conor** *seated.* **Fergus** *standing beside them and gathering of* **Red Branch Soldiers**, *including* **Felim**, *their leader.* **Conor** *rises to speak.*

Conor
We gather every Samhain and we mark
The death of darkness, the victory of light:
This night when past and present meet
And stretch new skin on future day.
A time to make amends, to scar old wounds,
To say: in this brief span of mortal being
We quell the jealous beat of mortal power,
A beat that some would say
Has overpowered my step;
Set it astray from where it should be placed –
Uniting old and young, sure of its path,
Leading all Ulster as my uncle did
When he was King. Tonight, his exile over,
Fergus returns to us from Connaught –
A flame come back from darkness:
My uncle and my father home.
Now let the Red Branch flower again,
Now let division heal and one strong limb
Be whole and healthy,
Long may it endure.

Ness
With joy we gather here tonight,
For the sake of Ulster and the start of a new day.
With joy we welcome home my husband:
Fergus, we lay our hopes before you –

May breathe with easy heart.
Felim, for its sake I'll stand beside the throne
And help my brother's son, my own flesh.
Help scar the wounded past
And see no knife will agitate that wound again.

The young, too, may rest easy:
Conor has won your loyalty –
And youth will make the future
Whether we lead or follow.
I'll not disturb what's here
Once I see it's honourable:
I won't unseat what's fairly done.

Here I stand. This Samhain night
We vanquish the dark days.

Conor *embraces* **Fergus**. **Fergus** *kisses him*. **Ness** *kisses both men. Applause.*

Conor
    Felim . . . (*Indicating that* **Felim** *is invited to speak.*)

Felim
    Fergus is home, and once content to be,
    Let all dissension pass;
    And in this hour let Ulster's men
    Pledge heart and sinew to their King
    And all who guide him well.

    My wife, in days or hours,
    Will bring new life to us.
    My son, I'm sure of it,
    Will be as true and brave
    As all the Red Branch are
    And have been and will be.
    He'll be born to this new order,
    He will see the infant years,
    The bright and steady steps
    Of Ulster's Kingdom
    Grown to new strength and power.

Applause.

Fergus
I call upon our King
To seal these pledges
And our hope,
A cup to what's to come.

Ness (*to* **Conor**)
The cup.

Conor *raises a cup to toast the night and peace.*

Conor
I raise this cup to Ulster and a new day.

All drink.

Now we watch the death of darkness:
Tell Cathach to begin.

Scene Two

Enter **Cathach**. *Two cages are brought in, each containing a huge sphere, one gold, one milky-grey silver. Or maybe the spheres are simply rolled in.*

Cathach
Who made these, the eggs of night and day?
And where were these eggs laid?
Who was mother to the darkness,
Who lay in fierce embrace to sire light?

Night had a black-winged mother,
She was courted by the wind,
And in the womb of nothing laid her egg.

Day's father saw what she had done
And wrestled down a wingless thing in flight;
She laid her egg next to the egg of night.

Contained in each, the force of light and dark;
Each force a bull, one black, one white;

Each Samhain gathers up their strength again,
To battle for all power.

Conor

Let loose the bulls.

The eggs open to release two men in bull costumes, the hides of bulls covering part of their naked bodies, the bull heads complete with horns. One man – the **Bull of Day** *– is painted white and his bull hide and head is white; the other – the* **Bull of Night** *– is black with black hide and head.*

Cathach

Which bull should die;
And which shall live?
Will darkness triumph
Over light?
Or should bright day
Beat down the dark;
The sun be radiant victor
And the moon quenched out?

The **Bulls** *paw the ground, walk around each other.*

Bull of Night

The night must live,
If she dies, so dies ease;
Your eyes, forever watchful,
Will grow blind with seeing;
Your mind will come
To curse the light and say

We should have heeded darkness,
We should have slaughtered day;
And now, too late, your sleep
A white and sickened thing,
And night a vanished memory:
No stars, no moon, no distant
Sparking fires to flame our hope
And wonderings;
No leather wings at dusk to brush
Our hair, no easeful shades of grey,

Or pale, or pitch or drifting black,
No rest for restless minds, the toss
And turn of troubles never soothed,
But magnified: the sullen bee of day
Entrapped in every skull.
Imagine only light-burnt skies:
If you choose the death of darkness,
The topple of this bull,
Then all hope dies.

Bull of Day
Think of living without day,
And think to live:
No dawn, no sun, no warmth,
No heat, no light;
Eternal shades of grey and black,
Eternal night; no mist, no dawn,
No birdsong and no dusk,
No rainbow hovered over shining lake,
No shadow – only shadow – no glint
Of silver on a fish's back.
Deny the claim of dark
That it would hold the moon and stars,
For what are they but light,
And if the bull of day is slain
Then night will lose its hopeful gleam;
The sky forever void and changeless,
A tomb to laughter and the busy world.

Who will find their way in endless dark
Without the spark of day to be their guide?
The feet and hands of work and play
Now dull and lazy, and the mind dulled too.
How many hours sleep can we endure
Before our eyes rebel? The caterpillar shell
Of life itself left in the dark to lie and rot.
Choose light – or in the darkness die.

The two **Bulls** *enact a short ritual battle. As the black bull seems to be gaining control,* **Conor** *steps between them and kills the black bull, who topples to the ground.*

Conor
> The darkness is defeated,
> Day is crowned.

Conor *hands a wreath to* **Fergus**, *who places it on the horns of the white bull. As he does, a cry is heard, a scream, a note unearthly, human, terrible.*

Conor
> What cry is this unnerves the Samhain night?
> No human sound.

Ness
> Not human:
> A wolf or stag defeated,
> Put to flight.

The cry is heard again.

Conor
> It cries again:
> What omened bird is this?
> Why is it here?

Ness
> No bird, no omen.
> Have no fear:
> The dogs have scented news of Cathach's kill.

Conor
> Maybe. And yet.
> We'll say no more of it.
> My friends, to peaceful life

He raises a cup to toast again. The loudest cry is heard.

Felim
> My wife in labour – her birth cries.

Ness
> The strangest sound I ever heard of woman.
> Or of man. Or even child. No, it's an animal.

Enter **Leabharcham**.

Leabharcham
Is Felim here?
Your wife would see you,
Come to her.

Felim *moves to leave.*

Conor
No, let her come here if she is able.
(*To* **Leabharcham**.) Is she fit?

Leabharcham *nods 'Yes'.*

Exit **Leabharcham***; re-enters with* **Felim's Wife***, frightened, upset.* **Felim** *goes to her.*

Felim
We heard your cry.

Conor
And never heard such pain before.

Felim's Wife
It wasn't me.

Ness
I said it. Feral sounds of night.

Felim's Wife
It would be relief to make those cries myself –
Or hear them calling from the darkened woods.
They come from in me – but not from me.
They come from what is yet unborn:
This womb is prison to a captive thing
I fear will take my life.
Each cry sucks out the sinew of my being.

Leabharcham (*to* **Felim**)
If you gain a fearful warrior you will lose a wife.

Felim
This cannot be.
How could I choose between two lives I love?
My woman, steadfast as an oak-tree in the forest –
My son, the seeded sapling of our hope.

Felim's Wife
 I have no choice. It cries again – but only in my flesh.

Ness
 This woman is a squealing boy –
 She's not the first to cower on the brink of birthing.

Fergus
 Not every woman has your strength.

Ness
 Each woman's strengthened by the life she bears.
 I cannot listen to this whining.

Fergus
 These cries are surely sent through from the gods.
 We'll hear their meaning.
 Cathach, have you read this night?

Cathach
 The skies have been too dark to read,
 So I killed a deer.
 (*To* **Felim's Wife**.)
 Will you let me feel what's there?

He puts his hands on her belly. Listens.

 A girl-child. She'll soon be in this world.
 (*To* **Leabharcham**.)
 You should take her now to be delivered.

Exit **Leabharcham** *with* **Felim's Wife**.

Felim
 You see it wrong. The child will be a boy.

Cathach
 You'll wish it so.

Fergus
 This cry we heard? What does it mean?

Ness
 Read the deer if that's what's to be done.

Cathach *brings in a golden dish with the entrails of a slaughtered deer to 'read' the portents of the baby's cry. He goes into a kind of trance, 'reads' the signs.*

Cathach
What signs are here?

What shape is brooding
Between flesh and bone?

What three hunters chase those fleeing lights?
And who's there in their wake, no, now ahead,
What prey or hunter,
Hair like strands of night?

What's here?
The muffled snow;
A deer, a raven,
The earth below all warm
With fallen flesh.

A thunder roll,
A chill east wind,
The storm's hum:
The air alive with ghosts
Of what's to come.

This cry tells siegeful towns and rafters burning,
Old women running from the sear of heat;
It brings a scurry plague of yellow vermin,
To raid the spilling entrails in the street.

It brings the clash of steel and stench of battle,
Betrayal, and a vulture-shrouded sky;
The rivers stained with shit and clot of bodies,
A thousand years of Ulster in that cry.

Great forests burned to clear more room for killing,
Swift pike and eel pick clean the drifting dead;
The red branch ripped like bone from tender socket,
A King brought down, all youth and mercy fled.

This girl-child in the womb will be of beauty
As cool as midnight moon, as hot as sun;
The stars will scatter dusting for her journey
And earth lament that journey when it's done.

Her name – Deirdre;
That name remembered when we are long forgot.
That name a warning –
Kill her tonight.

Ness
It must be done.
(*To* **Conor**.) Tell him.

Conor (*to* **Felim**)
You heard the omens:
Son or daughter,
Your child must die.

Silence and a staring match.

Enter **Leabharcham** *carrying baby. She goes to* **Felim**.

Leabharcham
Your wife has died,
My sister gone:
This is the life she bore,
A daughter –
Look, see her beauty,
The store of all you loved
And all you are.

Felim
I cannot bear to look at her,
Take her away.

Ness
Give her here to me.

Leabharcham
What do you all stare at?
She's a new-born infant,
Nothing less nor more.

Cathach
Let Ness take the baby.

Leabharcham *stares around at all the watching faces.*

Leabharcham (*to* **Cathach**)
What have you seen or said
To cause these human hawks
To stare as though I carried death,
Not life . . .

Conor
He saw enough for us to know
There is no choice.
You heard her cries –
They tell us of the ruin
She'll bring to Ulster.

Leabharcham
You haven't seen her:
Look how innocent she is.

Ness
Innocent as a new-born snake.

Fergus
Bring her here.

Leabharcham *brings the baby to* **Fergus**. *He looks at her. Holds her.*

Fergus
All have heard the word of Cathach.
Should she die, this child?

A loud murmer of 'Yes' through the hall.

Fergus
And 'yes' would seem what's right:
But pause and ask
Can we misread the signs?
Not what they say,
But what we cause by what we read
Of them and do.

So, if we kill this child
What do we bring?
Felim is heart-wounded now,
Might even welcome death
For this small one whose life
Has stilled the breath of her own mother.
But in a year or two what will he feel?
If we kill his daughter, we take a part of him,
And who knows what revenge he'll have.

Conor

Felim, is this so?

Felim

My heart is dead,
I cannot say.

Fergus

If the child lives, and woe is, indeed,
Her name and purpose,
Who knows what fates may intervene,
To shape her life and ours.
We cannot commit an evil act
To change the course of destiny.

I say the child should live.

Ness

Kill her.
She'll bring ruin to Ulster,
To this court, to the Red Branch.

Leabharcham

How could she bring ruin?
A baby, newly born.
Look at her:
How could you wish her harm?

Conor

Bring the creature here that I may see it
And its fearsome power.

Leabharcham *hands the baby to* **Conor**, *who cradles her, stares into her face.*

Conor
I see no wickedness:
I see no evil in these eyes.

Cathach
The evil lurks not in her –
But around her:
Her destiny here,
Written in this flesh.

Conor
So, fated infant, should you live or die?
Leabharcham – you mourn your daughter and your sister.
Should this infant live?

Leabharcham
I've heard no cause she should be killed.
(*To* **Cathach**.)
How could you think of it?
To kill this child when we have lost
Our own. My breasts have milk
To nurture life – and you would
Staunch life out.

Conor
You heard the cry:
Your husband lately scrabbling in the pulps of deer
Draws out a piece and tells us here is Deirdre,
Who shall bring great ruin to Ulster.

Cathach
And destruction to the King.

Conor
This baby will destroy me? This thing?
Look, she grips my finger and she smiles,
Not yet an hour old.
Is she swaddled tight? The night is cold.

Ness
I say kill her.

Conor (*to* **Leabharcham**)
And what do you say?

Leabharcham
If you have the will to spare her, scatter mercy,
Its crop may be this prophecy undone.

Conor
So runs my mind as runs a pulse between us:
This child is spared, let no one do her harm.

Ness
Fool. Fergus is wrong.
Don't heed him.

Fergus
The wise choice of a wise King.
It augers well for future days.

Conor
My wisdom is my own;
I don't need praise or telling.
Take this baby, Leabharcham. Rear her well.
She'll be the daughter you have lost.
Keep her from the sight of men.
If she grows to be the beauty Cathach says,
I'll marry her myself.

Felim, go now to your wife.

Exit **Felim** *and* **Leabharcham** *with baby.*

Conor
Enough sorrow. Men of Ulster – drink!
Cathach, you did well to warn us,
But bury all those twisted signs;
Clean your hands of morbid probing.
Put on the mask of moon and bring the evening in.

Exit all but **Fergus** *and* **Ness**.

Scene Three

Ness *and* **Fergus** *alone in the hall. He moves to touch her.*

Ness

Don't –
How could you see her spared,
A bitchling hardly born,
A screeching thing whose life may be our ruin.
You heard what Cathach said –
Maybe you want it, Conor downed.

Fergus

We carry our ruin with us and within us.
She's as innocent as any other.

Ness

And marry . . . Did you hear him utter 'marry'
With that creature in his arms.
What fool talk is that?

Fergus

Fool talk, maybe not.
Felim's daughter wed to Conor
Could be rock to this new Kingdom
That you seek:
The steady leader of the Red Branch
Kin to King, a King who needs
His uncle home to rule; whose
Weakness we know well, as do all
In this divided place. Each year breeds
More impatient bloods who'd make
New order for new order's sake.
That squealing thing you wanted dead
Might yet be our best future,
But the road ahead is long till then
And we must keep in step.

Ness

To tunes you make that mock me and my son?
'I'll not rehearse it all,'

And then you lay each word out
Like foundation stones
Of vengeance and our fall
Before the Red Branch.
We have to sit there through all,
Our faces masked in smile;
You knew we had no choice
But swallow down our anger.
I'd as soon you stabbed me in the heart,
One quick, clean, honest act.

Fergus

One quick, clean, honest act,
Like yours?

Truthful words?
'With all my heart I welcome Fergus home.'

Ness

I said those words before you spoke.

Fergus

Were you expecting praise for what you did?
My words were markers of my honour,
Small recompense for a throne.

Ness

You were a fool.
Did you think we'd give it back
When the year was gone?

Fergus

I was a fool:
I thought my brother's widow
Would be true.

Ness

True to her son.

Fergus

But not to me.
If this truce between us is to last,
If unity is what you want –

Along with power,
You'll be my wife.

Ness

If you'll be guardian to my son
And guide him well.

Fergus

My nephew, too – and King.

Ness

How cleverly you sing still.
How many women did you have in Connaught?

Fergus (*moving towards* **Ness,** *embracing, caressing her*)
Enough. But none as fine as you.
These years have served you well.
Did any other serve you, too?
Did you hire some young bull to keep you sated?
Was he as good as me?
Did he stroke your hair, your back, your legs,
And here . . .
Did you miss this?

Do you feel it?
The fire we made is still alight.
Have the embers died in you?

Ness *is silent. Does not respond to* **Fergus***'s love-making.*

Fergus

I know they're sleeping in your breast.

Ness

Then you learned nothing in your exile.
Five years I've known ease,
No man to meddle with my flesh;
No snoring body in my bed at night
To keep my sleep at bay.
I had no need of any man,
My hands can do his work,
Can play the body's tunes
Without his weight and sweat.

Such ease: if only every woman
Knew it.

Fergus
If only men knew women's minds:
And didn't need the rest of them . . .
We'd be wise fools.

Ness *pushes him away.*

Ness
Then be the first.
This is my mind:
I'll be your wife in public eye,
I'll stand beside you,
Stroke your hand and smile;
And all will say how well
We look together and how fairly
We resolved our wars.

I'll close my eyes to every bitch you bed,
Only keep their scent away from me
And never think to wed again,
Or make a son with any wife.

Fergus
I'd sooner make a son with you;
Only you'll have none but him.

Ness
I'll have no more:
The two I had sapped up
Enough of me.
Usna's brood are thriving:
They might devour us yet.

Fergus
Every life is a threat to you:
It's a wonder you can sleep
For fear of plots to pull you down.
And you'd have me a kind of eunuch
To your power:
What kind of life is that?

Ness
A life of ease.

Fergus
For you.
For me a torment,
All lies and make-believe.

Ness
A life as real as any other.

Fergus
As real as this?
As what the flesh can feel?

Fergus *grabs* **Ness** *again, holds her.*

Ness
The flesh is slave
To what the mind controls.

Fergus
Hard words:
But where's the hardness here?
This skin as soft as moss . . .

Ness
Moss drapes rock and stone
And hides it,
But the stone is hard.

Fergus
This is no stone, no rock,
No hard cliff-face,
No cave of ice and chill.
Feel how it melts,
Feel how the softness yields.

Ness
You think your breath
Would melt the winter?
Your hands would
Win the day?

Fergus
 Would win this night with you.

Ness
 Is this why you came back?

Fergus
 For this as much as Ulster.
 You know that well.
 And I'll have it.

Fergus *kisses* **Ness** *passionately. She responds slowly, almost dispassionately, then gives way, relishes the power of her body and her power over* **Fergus**. *They make love.*

Act Two

Scene One

Leabharcham *alone.*

Leabharcham
Cathach,
Where are you tonight?
So absent from me
My heart has left its bowl
And strayed away.
I search for it:
I see it in the moonlight,
The shape of you
And all my longing for you.
You stand beneath the oak,
When I reach it, you are gone;
I know the grass is warm
Where you have been.
I walk the pathway to the lake;
The trees are sentinels of Heaven,
But the gods of life have fled
And Heaven is an empty tomb.
I look into the water,
Your face is dabbling
Just within my reach.
My hand goes out to touch you,
And the water breaks between my fingers.
When it finds its calm again,
No face, not even mine,
No light, the moon as hidden now as you.

Sweet breasts,
Why do you feel this ache
When the heart is gone?
Why do my hungry hands
Stray on you to kindle a desire

That quenches even as it flares.
The mouth of love you'll never know,
The milk that should flow from you,
The paps of fun and joy trapped
On a hollow body.

If you were gone, cut off by fate,
He might stray to me.

If I had the power
To change shape I would:
I'd put aside this woman's flesh
And feelings,
Step into the ribs and skin of man,
Go haunting these same shadowed paths
By moonlight,
Find him, and lie down.

Then would my heart return,
And, in my boyish body,
Be my womb, and all my joy.

Enter **Cathach**.

Cathach
Where's Deirdre?

Leabharcham
You frightened me.
Why are you here so late?
She's sleeping.
What else would she do?

Cathach
Ness wants to see her;
Tomorrow, at the court.
You're to bring her
Hidden from all eyes.

Leabharcham
I wish she could be hid from Ness.

Cathach

It might be as well she were.
The King's in mourning;
His sister Usna's dead,
Her husband dying –
A sudden fever.

Leabharcham

The boys?

Cathach

Alive and well;
They were away
And didn't eat the food
Their parents ate,
Or breathe the wind
That brought disease –
Ness has a swift hand
And leaves no trace.
She'd be as happy
If the boys were dead.

Leabharcham

How can she hold such hatred?
To wish harm on her own . . .

Cathach

Ness's heart is small:
The one room in it 's filled by Conor;
Usna never saw its walls.
She looks at Naoise and she sees
A future rival to her son,
A warrior who might be King
Or lead a new King in if Conor falls.

Leabharcham

How could he fall
With Ness and Fergus at his side?

Cathach

They're out of step, all three:
There's discontent:

The young who worshipped Conor
Mutter that he grows disdainful of their word;
He raises taxes, drives away old friends,
Divides the loyalties of those he should bind in.
His heart and mind are hidden.

Leabharcham
The heart and mind can hide in men.

Why have you stayed away so long?
What have I done to be left alone?

Cathach
You're not alone:
Deirdre is here with you.

Leabharcham
Alone for you.

Cathach
Now is not the time.

Leabharcham
Never, never the time:
Never the time to talk,
Never the time for me.
Am I grown so old, so worn
That you'd rather stay away?
Would you sooner I was boy or man?

Cathach
How can you ask me that?

Leabharcham
Well, what's the truth?

Cathach
The King has need of me;
I must be gone.

Exit **Cathach**.

Enter **Child Deirdre**, *carrying a doll. She watches*
Leabharcham *for a moment.* **Leabharcham** *takes* **Child**
Deirdre *by the hand. They walk together.*

Scene Two

The **Child Deirdre** *and* **Leabharcham** *waiting for* **Deirdre**
to see **Ness**.

Deirdre
Why were you crying?
I thought that seeing Cathach made you happy.

Leabharcham
As seeing you, so full of beauty, does.

Deirdre
Did you cry because he left again?

Leabharcham
I can't remember if I cried at all.

Deirdre
You did. I heard.

Leabharcham
It must have been the rain
Sobbing at your window.

Deirdre
No, it was you.
Sometimes pain is very close to love.

Leabharcham
What did you say?

Deirdre
I said pain is close to love.
Well, isn't it?

Leabharcham
Who told you that?

Deirdre
No one. But I know.

A boy was in my dreams last night.
His hair was black.
His eyes were black.

His skin was very white.
I liked him.

He said words to me
But I couldn't hear.
He said his name
But I couldn't hear.

Do I have a brother?

Leabharcham
It's a dream.
We all imagine things in sleep.
You have no brother.

Say no more of it.
Is your dress straight? Turn around.
Say nothing of this dream to Ness.
Now, do your bow.

Deirdre *practises a bow.*

Leabharcham
And nothing of your thoughts:
Just smile, and yes, or no.
Agree with her.

Now go.

Deirdre *walks to meet* **Ness**. *Does not bow when she sees her.*
Leabharcham *may hover, unseen by* **Ness**, *watching the scene.*

Ness
Come, child,
No need to be afraid.
Bring your pretty doll.

Did Conor give you that?

Deirdre *nods 'Yes'.*

Ness
Look at its hair, just like your own.
This baub could be the very spit of you:
Blue eyes −

I wonder how they get that blue?
Did you know that sap of ivy
Mixed with salty water makes red dye?
A very sudden red:
They daub it on the cheeks
Of warriors going into battle,
And even when they're dead
They look alive.

Tell me,
Does Conor bring you many things?

Deirdre

Each time he visits he'll bring something.
He's very kind to me.

Ness

And when he visits,
Does he talk of anything?

Deirdre

Last time he talked of a great ship
He'd sailed in – and the sea.
He said the waves were taller
Than the oak outside
And the water tastes of salt –
It must be bitter then, to travel,
Though I think I'd like it.
He said he saw a mermaid.

Ness

Does he ever speak of me?

Deirdre *weighs this, pauses, looks at* **Ness,** *sizing her up.*

Deirdre

No.

Ness

Come closer, dear . . .

Ness *takes a reluctant* **Deirdre** *on her knee.*

Ness
  Did he ever play with you?
  Put you on his knee,
  Hug you like this,
  Kiss your hair . . . ?

Deirdre
  Are you a mermaid?

Ness
  Is it my dress, or hair, that makes you wonder?

Deirdre
  No, it's because you smell like a fish.

The two stare at each other, each taking the other's measure.

Ness *pulls* **Deirdre***'s hair.*

Ness
  Does that hurt you?

Deirdre
  No.

Ness *pinches* **Deirdre***'s arm sharply.*

Ness
  Or that?

Deirdre
  No.

Ness
  I could burn your hand in the fire.

Deirdre
  I can hold my finger in a candle flame.

Ness *pokes at the corner of* **Deirdre***'s eye.*

Ness
  Would it hurt if I put out your eye?

Deirdre
I'd still have the other one to watch with.
Anyway, you wouldn't do it:
The King would kill you.

Ness *sizes* **Deirdre** *up again. Recognises an equal. Smiles.*
Searches for a way to subdue her.

Ness
Look at your doll.

She snaps the doll in two.

This is what I'll do to you
If you ever harm him:
I'll break your back.
He means to marry you
And you'll do as well
As any other, maybe better.
No son of yours would be afraid
To lead and you'd bring a kind
Of beauty to our line.

But cross him – or cross me –
And you'll see your beauty
Scarred beyond all knowing;
People will say 'Deirdre'
When they mean a crawling,
Crippled thing, a torn bag-mask
For a face, a rag of hair,
Four twisted, flapping limbs,
Two teeth in a jagged smile.
They'd not put you out
To warn off scald crows.
Would you like that, Deirdre?

Deirdre
That will never be.

Ness
Not if you have wit enough
To see what can be yours;

Just keep a fetter
On your scheming mind.
I'll make this pact:
If you stand by my son,
Marry him and bear
My grandchild, I'll stand
Behind your throne
And tolerate you;
You'll live to see me buried.

Make mischief,
And *your* tomb is ready waiting.

Do you hear me?

Deirdre

Yes, I do.

Ness

Then good.
Now go and play.
Tell Leabharcham
To come to me –
We'll make this doll like new.

Scene Three

Eamhain Macha. A gymnasium or training ground. **Naoise**, **Ainle**
and **Ardan**, *young warriors, are training – maybe wrestling.* **Conor**
and **Cathach** *watch them.*

Conor

Your eyes enjoy this sight;
I see it in them . . .

Cathach

Who could deny how pleasing
The view of youth
From the hilltop of mid-life.

Conor

And some it pleases more than others.
Each leap, each stretch, each catch,
Each graceful fall.

But still, your eye is brightest
When my nephews take the field.

Cathach

They're swift and pleasing;
I'll not deny it.

Conor

Naoise above all.

Cathach

And Ardan . . .
All three, Ainle . . .

Conor

Ah, Ardan!
Such thighs, such arms, such strength,
Who'd not rejoice to see them?
But best to keep the feasting
To your eyes.
Then no one is dishonoured.

They watch the young men in silence for a little.

Conor

My mother thinks that Naoise grows too strong:
She wants me to subdue him.

Cathach

Naoise will be loyal so long as you are just.

Conor

She thinks without a son of mine to groom
He could rise up the soldiers, take the throne.

Cathach

It's true he's favourite to them all
And that could be his power.

Conor
Did you go?
Did you see them?

Cathach
Last night.

Conor
And told them to expect me?

Cathach
Everything you say, I do.

Conor
How was she?

Cathach
She doesn't grow more ugly
Or any less a woman.

Conor
How fast the years flee with us:
The time has come.

Bring Fergus in,
I think his mind dwells on just the same.

Exit **Cathach**. **Conor** *claps his hands to stop the training.*

Conor
Stop! Enough. Rest up! (*Calls* **Naoise** *forward.*)
Naoise, walk with me.

Naoise *walks forward, the others rest.*

Naoise
Uncle, King . . .

Conor
Watching you is like the memory of my youth
Made brighter and bigger by the sun.
It pleases me to watch you grow to manhood.

Naoise
I hope I'll be the man my father was:

I honour his memory, and my mother's
Every day.

Conor

As I do. As you should.

Naoise

As my brothers do.

Conor

Good. But I don't want you to outgrow your youth
Too fast or forget the easy joys of hunt and play.
Enough of body's lust for strength and battle;
Put away your weapons; let today be the start
Of time you can enjoy. A month away from it,
A month of ease to wander free in Ulster –
What I'd give to go with you . . .

Naoise

We can't –
The Games are in two weeks,
We're champions now,
We'll lose face if we're away.

Conor

Not when it's known I ordered you to rest.

Naoise

They'll not like it.

Conor

They? Your brothers –
Or the young who think they know it all?

Naoise

I only ask for fairness.
As young or old would ask
And expect that they'd be given.

Conor

Would expect that they'd be given what they want?
Not do what they're ordered?
What King – or army – could stand for that?

Naoise

I ask you, please, don't do this.
Have I been disloyal to you?

Conor

Your loyalty's rewarded
With a month of freedom.
No more of it:
Tell your brothers the good news.
Go.

The two stand facing each other, a small face-off, then **Naoise**
obeys and goes to his brothers. Enter **Fergus**. *He and* **Conor**
watch the brothers confer, look towards them, continue training briefly,
then exit.

Fergus

Your nephews are handsome youths.
They'll please the eye of all
Who watch the Games.

Conor

They'll please no eye these Games
And win no prize.
I'm sending them to rest –
To hunt and take their ease.
Then their heads won't grow too wild
With leafy crowns and crowds to cheer them.

Fergus

You can't do this:
Naoise's set to be a champion.
It'll turn the young against you.

Conor

So he said too:
'They'll not like it.'
Now 'You can't.'
It seems a King
Is not the master
Of his mind – or Kingdom.

Fergus
I'm here to be your guide,
A kind of strength beside you:
They're her words;
A pillar to your weakness:
They're mine.
Not here to put my mark
On every foolish act,
Or mutter constant 'Yes'
With a clenched smile.
Send off your nephews
If the sight of them displeases
But don't expect that I'll approve it.

Conor
I expect your loyalty
As I asked – and got – from Naoise.
They have to learn the shape of order
As well as the shape of strength and victory.
That's all that's to it,
I'm proud of them:
My sister's sons are almost sons to me.

Fergus
Then treat them fairly.
Don't force them to lose face.
Naoise's the finest soldier in his rank,
Every man in every regiment talks of them.
Dishonour them and you dishonour all.

Conor
There's no dishonour in obeying orders:
They'll not dissent from what they're ordered to do.
No others will dissent unless they're groomed to it.

Fergus
You scatter dangerous seed on fertile ground.
There's discontent out there:
Each other day brings restless words –
Your taxes have sent tempers high,
You've grown too distant from the men,

They think you favour one and not the other;
Divisions flourish fast and strong as summer weed.

Conor

That's always so.

Fergus

But now you nurture it:
You think you show your strength
In what you do,
But this move could make you weak
And strengthen them.

Conor

Their strength is mine.
And I'll be stronger still
When I have Deirdre's son:
Felim's grandchild,
Yours too – as good as.
The sight of Deirdre at my side
Will unite the young
And draw them round me.

Fergus

Are you grown so far from them
That you think this?
It's the very thing they fear.
They know that she's of age,
They say your taxes go
On gifts for her, on lavish rooms,
A wedding feast like none before.
They know the stories of her:
Cathach's words of omen
Haven't lessened in the telling.
They think she'll bring destruction with her.

Conor

They're fools. And they're disloyal.

Fergus

Fools or not, it's how they think.
Win their loyalty.

You need to marry, yes.
But not Deirdre.

Conor

I'll marry her.
They'll not tell me what to do.

Fergus

Hear me . . .

Conor

Nor will you.
You're not my father
And won't tell me how to be.

Fergus

I'm not, nor would I wish it:
But I'll speak my mind.
If you'd had a father
You'd not be so weak.

Conor

You've not seen my strength.

Fergus

I've glimpsed enough of it
To know its shape.
Hear me out:
I know you see her.
I know that she's the beauty Cathach told.
We spared her life; we were right to spare her;
I used to think your sudden words that night
Might be foretellings of the future's store:
A marriage to unite all Ulster, a barrier to war.
Now I see the danger Cathach saw,
I know it in the men's unease and murmurings.

I said, that night, we can't commit
An evil act to alter destiny;
But don't invite disaster in.

You need an heir, you're right:
Without a son you make your nephew stronger.

But find another – take a different wife;
Felim's not so thought-of now
That his daughter's hand would
Strengthen what you have.
Other daughters might. Find one,
Make children with her.
It doesn't stop you having Deirdre,
She can't go anywhere
Or belong to anyone but you.
Keep her, use her.
But don't marry her: You'll bring down ruin.

Conor

If you saw her you'd not say that;
She's more than beauty –
She's a child still in her heart
And when the soldiers see her
They'll forget this talk of fate
And death and darkness.
You'll forget.

I remember nothing when I see her;
There's only now and what's to come.

Exit **Fergus**, *passing the young* **Deirdre**, *who's walking towards*
Conor. **Fergus** *doesn't see her.*

Scene Four

Conor *and* **Deirdre** *in the place where she has been raised.*

Conor

I open up my eyes and see the moon before me.
You look more radiant with each passing day.
Stand with your cheek to me, to the north light,
That I may see you better.

He watches her.

Now, come and sit on an old King's knee.

Deirdre (*teasing, coquettish*)
Not so old . . .
But I'm too old now for such child's games.
I beg your leave, don't ask me.

Conor
Nothing is asked that cannot be.
Come, new games are found
When children grow.
You'll see how joyful they can make the heart.
And, as once I bought you childish things –
A doll of ebony, a little castle with a King and Queen,
A new dress made of Grecian silk,
So now, new games need richer outcome –
(*Producing a gold necklace.*)
The best gold from the finest goldsmith.
Your wedding gift from me.

Deirdre *does not react, walks forward. He puts the necklace on, sits her on his knee, feels her breasts.*

Conor
How these flowers have grown –
From the smallest seedlings that the eye could see.

Deirdre
Do they please this King?

Conor
Does the scent of meadow clover please the bee?

Deirdre
Then please the flower as the bee must do –
Kiss me.

He kisses her, a little awkwardly, almost roughly.

Deirdre
Gentler. Gentler.
Does the bee in taking pollen sting the flower?

She kisses him.

Conor
If I did not know better I'd swear you older –

More a woman than a maid.

Deirdre
Can't a maiden have a woman's feelings?

Conor (*suspicious, jealous*)
Who stirred this first?
I doubt this game is not the first you played.

Deirdre (*breaking away from him*)
And who would I have played with, fettered here
Like a doe for King Stag's breeding?
Where would I have seen a man but you?
Do you think I kissed with Cathach?
Do you think in all the blue of sky
That is roof to my unfreedom
I made a man of stars or cloud or sun
And brought him down to lie with?

Shun me then, if you think such thoughts;
But if you shun me, set me free –
Release me from this cage of bondage;
Give me back my life; let me *see* life.

Conor
Soon enough and all is yours to view:
Your spirit well befits a queen for Ulster;
Come – I should not have doubted you.

What – will you not kiss me now?

Deirdre
Let you kiss me.

He kisses. She holds back, cold.

Conor
In seven days you come to Eamhain Macha,
In seven days you walk arrayed in red;
With gold aglint on every tress and finger,
In seven nights we share a wedding bed.

Exit **Conor**.

Act Three

Scene One

Deirdre *and* **Leabharcham**.

Deirdre

I'll not do it;
I'll not marry him.
He's too old and I'm too young.
He can keep his gold.

*She flings **Conor**'s present from her.*

What have I done
To earn this?
Confined to here,
Locked in from life –
A plaything for a King;
Then shackled in Eamhain Macha,
A placid glinting thing
To breed sons for Ness and him.

Leabharcham

You've done nothing:
You can't help your beauty;
He can't help but see it
And want it for his own.

Deirdre

Maybe if I marked my face he'd leave me;
Days I swear I'd scar this flesh
To see his hands recoil.
I want to know the world outside of here.
I want to live.
I won't go to Eamhain Macha.

Leabharcham

What choice is there?
There are worse fates
Than to be his Queen.

Deirdre
No worse fate now for me:
Seven days before I'm tied to him,
Seven days –
I'd sooner die.

Leabharcham
You say you want to live
And now you'd die.

Deirdre
This marriage would be death.
You don't know how I fear it:
The sheets turned back,
His body next to mine,
That grizzled face upon me;
His breath like mildew at my ear.
He's too old!
I'll turn ancient in his arms,
Grow cold and worn:
What use is gold then?

Leabharcham
He's King,
And he's not so old;
I smelt his breath myself,
It's clear and clean.

Deirdre
Then you were not as close as I have been!

They laugh.

Help me Leabharcham,
Please help me . . .

Leabharcham
What is there I can do?
You have to marry him,
I'll be with you at Eamhain Macha.
You can't spurn him:
Women would die – or kill – to fill your shoes;
Think what it will be to be his wife!

Deirdre
I think of nothing else:
I know my life is over if I wed –
Those fools can have my shoes and chains!

Beat.

I dreamt of him again last night . . .

Leabharcham
Stop. I don't want to hear.

Deirdre
He was hunting with two others;
    It was winter.
The deer was young and lithe.
    The snow
Was everywhere, great branches
    Silent in the white of day.

They cornered her upon the crest of Manaun,
    Her fawn cried in a hidden slope;
She was dappled with the light
    Of autumn appling,
She was trembling, with his hands
    Upon her throat.

A thread of blood runs round;
    The stitch unravels,
Her head held back, his grip
    A tautened bow:
He draws the thread again,
    The main knot severs –
Her life pours hot and staining in the snow.

Leabharcham
You should hate him – this killer.

Deirdre
How could you hate a raven of such beauty?
Black hair, snow-skin, such lips
    Of rowan-red;

The deer swooned in his arms
    And died exalted.
If such a man is flesh
Our bed will be forever wakeful.

And then I think of Conor . . .
Better dead.

Leabharcham
Strange love that kills
And leaves a fawn unmothered;
Strange-hearted deer
That loves the killer's eyes;
Strange eyes that dream all this
And conjure passion.

Deirdre
Strange life that locks and smothers passion's cries.

Leabharcham
The gods forgive me:
I shouldn't tell you this −
His name is Naoise,
Conor's sister's son,
Son to Usna
Whom Ness hated.
Both their parents gone.

Deirdre
He lives?
Where can I see him?

Leabharcham
In this life:
Close as your dream.
He is alive and flesh
And hunting with his brothers
In the hills.
Walk east three miles at daybreak;
Time you saw the light beyond these walls.

Deirdre
>Naoise. Naoise.
>His very name is beauty.

Leabharcham
>As a mirror knows itself;
>So beauty looks on beauty – and may die.

Deirdre
>Well gloomy weather, cast a cloud on joy!
>First you raise my heart, and then you pull it down;
>I won't listen.

Leabharcham
>Too well I know that.
>I'm a fool –
>I shouldn't have given in;
>He's kin to Conor
>So the cut will go more deep.
>These years, since you were small,
>These dreams of him.

Deirdre
>Since I was seven.

Leabharcham
>These years I kept a tight grip on my tongue.
>And would have held it still
>But to see you young – and you –
>And searching for your second soul,
>For that's what love can be.
>
>If you were happy I'd not mind,
>Though, to see you tied to Ness . . .

Deirdre
>That bind will never be.

Leabharcham
>You're wise enough to know
>That my heart aches for what is not;

And nights I've wept; no rain
But my sad storm.

And I think of you and Conor . . .

O, my Deirdre, I'd not do you harm
For all the world,
Yet maybe that's what I have done.

Deirdre
Only the harm of freeing me.
'Naoise'.
Now I know the name of freedom.

Leabharcham
And freedom sets its traps
Where lovers run.
Search for him, find him,
Know was this your dream.
Be back by evening
Or see freedom gone.

Exit **Deirdre**. *Enter* **Cathach**.

Cathach
Where is she?

Leabharcham
Safe. Flown.

Cathach
Flown to where?
Where is she gone?

Leabharcham
Maybe to where you go at night:
Tracking the paths you follow
To find a warrior.
Every songbird finds its own.

Cathach
She knows of Naoise . . .
You've told her.

Leabharcham
No. She told *me* of *him*:
For years she dreamt him,
I had no choice but tell her
What she knew.

Cathach
She didn't know it,
And might never have
But for your loose tongue.

Have you no heed
For what you've done?

Leabharcham
I've been starved of love;
I'll not see her famished
Or tied to a body
She'd grow to hate.

Cathach
Though hate is what you're calling down,
A hate as strong as love.
You've set fate loose:
Death will be forging steel from this,
Will you be happy then?

Leabharcham
My happiness is hers
And not my own.

Scene Two

*Sound of hunting horn. Morning mist drifting. Figures caught sight
of:* **Naoise**, **Ainle**, **Ardan** *hunting.* **Deirdre** *moves around,
watching the brothers, unseen by them. They may wrestle, echo the
earlier training scene from Eamhain Macha.*

Deirdre *lies down and strokes her ankle, as if she has sprained it.
We hear a cry, a mingling of* **Deirdre**'s *pre-birth cry and the cry of*

a deer. **Naoise** *becomes aware of it, listens, moves towards the sound.*
Ardan *and* **Ainle** *move off, exit.*

Naoise *reaches* **Deirdre***'s side; the two gaze at each other.*

Naoise
> In all my days of hunting
> My eyes have never seen
> A sight more lovely.

Deirdre
> I fell, I hurt my foot.

Naoise
> Then let me tend to it.

He kneels to stroke her ankle, stares at her. In a short while **Deirdre**
maims or cuts **Naoise***.*

Naoise
> Why do I feel all this took place before?
> That we met here – or two
> Who had our spirits and our eyes?
> All life is stilled:
> I feel I could stretch out my hand
> And touch the skin of time.

Deirdre
> You saw me in a dream.

Naoise
> Yes. This is the dream.
> I see you now.

Deirdre
> No. This is life.
> Your hand upon my skin.

Naoise
> Did you dream it, too?

Deirdre
> I knew that what I saw was real;
> Not bright shadows of a sleeping mind.

Naoise
And you fell upon the earth this morning . . .

Deirdre
For you to find.

They embrace, kiss. Birdsong is heard.

Deirdre
What bird is that?
I have never heard so sweet a sound in all my life before.

Naoise
How could you hear?
Love's door was shut and bolted,
The hallway cold inside.

That song the green bird sings is only heard
When lover and beloved are one:
Two souls, one body,
Two fish swimming eye to eye,
Two hearts with single beat,
Beloved lip to lip,
Beloved thigh to thigh.

Deirdre
Who gave you this sweet tongue?

Naoise
It's not mine, it's yours;
Take it –
Bite it to the root

Deirdre
And sever love?
No, instead this fire –
Do you feel it?
Here – and here – and there.

Naoise
Yes.
How quick the flame,
How hot the hand's desire.

Deirdre
I am the huntress:
You are the deer,
I creep to where you lie:
I pounce . . .

Naoise
And so I die.
My neck is yours,
My heart, my haunch;
Feel here the pulse of passion.

Deirdre
Feel here the teeth of love.

Naoise
And so . . .

Deirdre
And so . . .

Naoise
And so . . .

They make love . . .

Scene Three

Ness *cursing, on her knees before some pre-Christian image or altar; maybe using cursing stones. Hair down and combing it.*

Ness
Sun burn them up
Earth dig a grave for them
Moon pull the sea
Onto the rocks for them
Night hide the way
Darkness be guide to them
Shorten their day
Skin be a shroud for them

Skin be a shroud to them
Shorten their day
Darkness be guide for them
Night hide the way
Onto the rocks for them
Moon pull the sea
Earth dig a grave for them
Sun burn them up
Onto the rocks . . .

She looks up, sees **Fergus** *watching her.*

Ness
Now look what your mercy's done.
I knew it in my bones that cursed night,
She should have died if our hopes were to live.

Fergus
Is that how you read for me?
How you won my weakness?
And for Usna?
Put away those things:
Stand by your son,
For once he has a need of you.

Exit **Fergus**. **Ness** *remains kneeling, 'praying' silently.*

Scene Four

Deirdre
Naoise,
I knew you before I ever met you,
Before my eyes caught sight of you
I knew your soul.
Do you think me mad?
As the bole of a tree and the branch are one
I knew you,
Every leaf of your body,
Every scar of your back,

Every songbird nesting in your highest branches.
What is this feeling?
A power running through me
Like the surge of hounds to hare.

It is a joyous demon
Who has found my eyes
And made the world new through seeing
With a laughing mind.

It is a stream of silver fish
Shoaling, dabbling in the morning light;
It is the moon, a yellow lantern in the heart.
It is a field of stars, the night an endless flower,
And you the scent.

Naoise

It's a lot.

Deirdre

Do you not feel it too?

Naoise

I do.

Deirdre

Why so silent then?

Naoise

Men are not so apt to talk as you;
It does not mean we do not feel, or love.

I also think – how harsh the gods are,
How their games with man are cruel;
From above it seems they look at us below
As a heartless child looks on a summer track
And stamp and scatter life like dust and crawlers
And laugh to see us scurry here and back
And kick again when we are seeming settled,
Then, bored and hot, walk on with not one wrack
Of thought or care for what's undone.

Deirdre

Why do you speak like this just now, when we have met?
You'd swear you thought our meeting ill:
Better our paths had never crossed
Than you regret the moment in the moment's wake.

Naoise

How could I regret this joy?

Deirdre

Then how do you speak of cruel gods?
The gods who brought us here today.

Naoise

The gods who named you Deirdre:
Who wrote your fate, and maybe mine
In stars the night that you were born.
You could be no other with your beauty.

Deirdre

Deirdre is my name.

Naoise

And you know I am Naoise,
Sister's son to Conor,
Blood to him and kin.
If he were dead tomorrow
And Fergus put aside
Ulster would be mine.

I'm a soldier in the Red Branch;
Conor's already on his guard for insurrection,
I've watched his watching eyes – seen his stare,
He fancies danger where there isn't any,
He sees plots in every shadowed corner
And ghosts where only humans are.

Deirdre

What's that to us?

Naoise

Nothing – only life itself.

What do you imagine?
That I go to him and say
'Deirdre, who would be your wife
Is now my woman.
We didn't mean it,
The fickle gods above
set our paths together and we met;
The hours of passion since would fire Ulster.
We would be together, as the lark would be with morning,
And we beg your leave to marry,
To settle here among our people.
Perhaps you could find it in your heart
To give us land, not much, a thousand acres,
And a small command for me.
You could be second father to our children –
Think how happy you would be to see us happy . . . '
Well, is that how you foresee it?

Deirdre
I see nothing but you.

Naoise
Then you will quickly grow short-sighted –
But more likely blind.
What do you think – if he found us here?

Deirdre
He'd kill us.

Naoise
And you are happy then?
This course to death – the course you'd have us steer?

Deirdre
This day I could face death if you died with me.

Naoise
I'd sooner both of us might live.

Deirdre
Then let us leave from here.

Naoise
And where would give us welcome?

Deirdre
I don't know the world –
But there must be shelter there.

Naoise
Would you shelter with me?
Let me be a shelter to you
And you be sun and shade to me?
I'd sooner that than Ulster.
Sooner we be free together
For however short a day
Than parted from you now,
Who feels like twin to me:
As my sweet brothers are.
Twin oaks who'll stand beside us
In the face of love,
In the face of hate,
In the face of war.

Ardan *and* **Ainle** *draw in close to them.*

Deirdre
No need to fear of Conor's rage . . .

Naoise
No need – but best to fear:
Love's steed is swift,
Sure-footed in the moonlight;
We'll spur her gentle flanks with urgent heel;
We'll sight the sea by noonday,
Sail by evening –
Fate steer its course,
The gods do as they will.

Deirdre *and* **Naoise** *stand, flanked by* **Ardan** *and* **Ainle**.
Exit all.

Scene Five

The Hall at Eamhain Macha. **Fergus**, **Felim**, **Ness** *and* **Conor***; consternation in the wake of the news of the elopement of* **Deirdre** *and* **Naoise**. **Cathach** *leads* **Leabharcham** *in to their interrogation.*

Conor (*to* **Leabharcham**)
How did she learn of him?
Why was she not confined?

Leabharcham
Young feet will stray beyond confinement's gate.

Fergus
Then older hands should lock and bar their way,
How did she, confined and in your care,
Hear of him?

Ness
Was it out of air she drew his name?

Leabharcham
Yes, out of air, night's breath;
She conjured him in dreams.
For years she dreamt him,
Clear as you are now to me.
She says what does it mean,
This dream and who is he,
Describing clear as you,
Naoise's eyes, Naoise's hair,
Naoise's brow;
Years it happens,
Years and months
She questions, presses and torments.
What was I to do?

Conor
You told her.

Leabharcham
Only his name,
And that he lived.

Fergus
His name, alone,
Did not lead her to him.
How did she know the place to find him?

Leabharcham
They found each other:
What's 'place' to love?
A footstep left or right,
The path would be as true.

Ness
Who set her on this path, but you?

Leabharcham
Me? A drifting dust-mote in the house of time.
Another voice would say his name some other day;
Another day would bring their certain light.

Conor (*to himself*)
And just as certain night to me.

I should have killed her then,
Or had him killed.
I should have known their paths would cross;
(*To* **Cathach**.) Why did you not see it in the signs?
My nephew and the one who'd be my wife,
How did you not see it?

Cathach
It must be this I saw,
But didn't know.
There were three hunters,
But I didn't see.

Fergus (*to* **Conor** *and aimed at* **Ness**)
The three were hunting
Because you sent them off;
Away from victory,
From all that was their due.
You set their paths together;
Now you know the price

Of wielding power:
It needs a steady hand,
Not one that lashes out
When she commands it.
You wouldn't heed me.
See what her words have done.

Ness
It was her. (*Aimed at* **Leabharcham**.)
She brought them to each other.
No one else to blame.

Conor
I hear their laughter everywhere.
They're mocking me,
All of Ulster laughs.
(*To* **Leabharcham**.)
You caused all this,
You made them laugh at me. (*Hits her.*)

Enter **Red Branch Soldiers**.

Conor
Hunt them down:
Leave no place unburned
Where they might hide.
Give no one peace
Who'd shelter them.
Root out their closest friends
And make them hostage to their life or death.

I want them back alive.
I want her back.

Exit **Red Branch Soldiers**.

Conor (*to* **Leabharcham**)
Has she left anything behind?
I'd have some keepsake:
Something with the scent of her,
To fill my mind with rage
And then with calm.

Cathach
Give it to him.

Leabharcham *hands* **Conor** *the gold necklace he gave to*
Deirdre. **Conor** *holds it, looks at it, throws it from him.*

Conor (*to* **Cathach**)
Out. Out. Take her away from me.
Take her away.

Exit **Cathach** *and* **Leabharcham**. **Conor** *pounds his head*
against his joined fists, half-sobs, half-chokes, all anger, humiliation,
sorrow. **Ness** *comes to comfort him, puts her arms around him; he*
pushes her away. She picks up the necklace.

Conor
Deirdre, Deirdre.
I'll kill him:
I'll cut off his hands,
Put out his eyes
With his own thumbs,
So beyond the grave
He will be blind
And never see her.
They'll have the peace
Of rabid dogs driven
Here and there: hated,
Hunted, stoned and mocked.
I want her back.
She will come back to me.

Fergus (*to* **Ness**)
Now see your King.
See how wise you've made him.
Is this what I'm to stand behind
And give my name to?

Ness
Your wisdom had her spared:
We should have had her killed that first night.
But for you we would have.

Conor

It was Naoise should have died:
Why did none of us see that?

Felim

No one should have died
After that first death:
My wife, whose life was half
My own. The gods did this
Because I turned my back on life.
I should have taken Deirdre in my arms,
Reared her as the daughter that she is
And been a father to her.
She'd have met with Naoise
As small girl meets small boy
And none of this would happen.

Fergus

No joy now from wishing acts undone.
They met each other and they're gone.
The future's here before us, look at it:
A raving mind that must be calmed
Before the tide of vengeance washes in.

Act Four

Scene One

Scotland. **Ardan** *and* **Ainle** *act out a mock bullfight.* **Deirdre** *encourages them. She waves a piece of tapestry or sewing like a matador's flag.*

Deirdre
Bad bulls, bad bulls!
Back, back, back!

They withdraw reluctantly, paw the ground, snort.

Deirdre
When I wave this, attack.
It's a battle to the death.
Even if I beg you to stop,
Pay no heed to me.

Whoever wins, I'll stroke and treasure;
Whoever loses, (*Draws her hand across her throat.*)
His head upon that wall.

Deirdre *waves the cloth.*

Go!

The two brothers/bulls bellow, glare at each other, attack, clash heads, retreat; bellow, paw the ground, advance, clash. One begins to gain ground, pushes the other back, then loses ground, is pushed back; they sway to and fro, **Deirdre** *urging them on.*

Deirdre
Faster! Don't give in! Quick.
Watch to the left. To the right.
Too slow. Too slow.
Fight for Ulster! Fight for me!
Yes, Ardan, Yes, you're gaining on him,
In now, in now. Go, go, go.

Ardan *defeats* **Ainle**, *pretends to gore and kill him.*

Ardan
> Now I claim my wreath and kiss.

Deirdre *crowns him with the cloth she had been waving. Kisses him.*

Ainle (*from 'dead' on the ground*)
> And the bull who's dead would be kissed back to life.

Both **Deirdre** *and* **Ardan** *throw themselves on him, kiss him, all laughing. The three lie together, at ease, happy.*

Deirdre
> What was the thing of greatest beauty in your life?

Ainle
> Our mother's smile at night when we were boys.

Ardan
> The same. And the faces of my brothers.

Deirdre
> I never knew my mother,
> Though Leabharcham is my mother.
> Still, I sometimes think and wonder
> Who she was and who my father is.

Ainle
> The greatest beauty you have seen?

Deirdre
> Naoise.

Ainle
> And place – what place in Ulster?

Deirdre
> I only know the sky of it!
> Is it as lovely as they say?

Ardan
> No words of mine could tell it:
> When we return you'll see.

Deirdre
> Return?

Ardan

Oh, we *will* go back.
It has to be.

Ainle

Naoise wouldn't live
If this exile were for ever.
His heart is there.

Deirdre

Naoise's heart is me.

*The sound of a hunting horn is heard. The three get to their feet, wait.
Enter* **Naoise**.

Naoise

They're here.

Deirdre

Are we to move again?
I can't endure it.

Naoise

They're in the valley.
They'd be on us before day.

Deirdre

Can't we stay?
Can't you fight them?
They won't defeat the three of you!

Ardan

There are some we wouldn't wish to kill.

Deirdre

But they'd kill you.

Ainle

Some might. But others, no.

Naoise

How do you think I got the word they're here?
We've friends among them;
They'd sooner we'd be gone.

Deirdre
You'd sooner go with them – to Ulster!

Naoise
I'll not deny the moments I'm forlorn for it
And for our friends.
But don't deny my word and trust.
My place is where you are.
Do you doubt it?

Deirdre
No.

Naoise
Then end this doubtful talking:
Pack again to go.

Scene Two

Felim *and* **Fergus** *petition* **Conor** *and* **Ness** *in the court at Eamhain Macha.* **Cathach** *and* **Leabharcham** *may be present.* **Ness** *wears the necklace* **Conor** *gave to* **Deirdre**.

Fergus
If Naoise dies
The Red Branch breaks in two.
The sons of Usna are well loved:
Many men would die beside them,
Or take the part of honoured vengeance
If they come to a dishonoured death.

Conor, hear these words.
Hear them for *yourself.*
You've been deaf to me;
Heed Felim.

Felim
Ulster is divided: you know this.
The Red Branch want the sons of Usna back;
They're your kin, as brave and noble

As your father was; as brave and noble
As they'd be, being kin to you;
Your nephews whom you love.

Ness

Love! His nephews who betrayed him,
Who dishonoured him.
The only way they should return:
The dust and ashes of a common pyre,
Or bring their severed bodies home
To show they're dead;
To show the soldiers who might follow them
Where that fool path would lead.
To show who's King.
They know the price of what they've done.

Fergus

The price all Ulster pays:
The fire lit by vengeance burns still,
There's hardly one who hasn't felt its singe;
Each house where rumour had them sleep
Now lies in ashes;
Each pair of hands that might have offered help
Or food or nothing but what mind imagined
Shackled now;
Their loyal friends made guilty, division
Forged and strengthened on this maddened anvil.

Don't you see you hammer out the steel of war?
What reason might have understood,
The heart's fast kick against the walls of hurt,
Is magnified into such acts as call for vengeance back;
As nurture hate; as build a quiet will to see you downed,
And those who wronged you put there in your place.

Ness

That will never be.

Fergus

Not if you're wise and act to stop it.
They must be given pardon;

Allow them to return.
Pay recompense for the ruin you've done.
Show the men of Ulster that your power
Is more than might;
Show them that it has its roots in mercy;
That your sight has cleared again and sees
The unjust trail your heart had led you down.

Felim

Bring your nephews home, let them swear
A public oath of loyalty to you;
Make just settlement all round, bind them
In a fair and firm grip; let their place within
The Red Branch be enough to keep their honour;
Not enough to let them grow in power.

Fergus

Do this and Ulster stays united;
You'll win respect again,
Build a place of pride instead of enmity.
But let this war on them continue
And its borders will shrink back
Until you're circled round with no way out,
With all that Cathach saw that Samhain night
Made real – by you and not by Deirdre.

Conor

There's only one way to stop the growth of power:
To cut the root of it.
We saw what mercy brings.

Ness

How could you think to pardon what they've done?

Felim

They're your own kin:
Your grandsons, Ness;
Conor, these aren't strangers,
They're your sister's sons.

Conor

They're worse than strangers now:

My own blood gone bad;
It must be drained away.

Felim

I know I may be out of turn,
I know I've little right
To speak of love or recall
To anyone the bonds of kin.
I turned my head away
From my own daughter;
I am more to blame
Than she or Naoise
For what's come to pass.

I would undo the years
And hold her now,
A babe in arms
If such could be.

You showed her mercy then,
When she was born;
Extend that mercy now
And bring her home
With your three nephews
Whom you love.

Fergus

If seeing them would be
Too bitter yet,
Extend the word of pardon:
Let them live in peace
In Scotland,
And in the softened light
Of passing days,
Return when you're at peace.

Silence. **Conor** *seems away in thought.* **Ness** *watches him.*

Ness

We'll hear no more.

Conor *stirs out of thought.*

Conor
>When I'm at peace
>I'll think on it.

He gestures for **Fergus** *and* **Felim** *to leave. They exit.* **Ness** *goes to him, holds him in her arms.*

Ness
>You'll not heed them:
>You're my son and have my strength.
>Why should we trust in them?
>Who's to say what plots they're hatching,
>What they'll do when Naoise's back.
>All this suited Fergus –
>To let you run on blind into the storm,
>With him beside you, now behind, now
>Whipping up the wind to blow you down.
>It's not for love of you or me he wants them back.
>He never forgave us taking Ulster's throne.
>Felim is her father, and smitten with remorse.
>They'd have all Ulster for themselves;
>They'd not show us any mercy.

Conor
>What am I to do?
>I want her still.

Ness *whispers in* **Conor**'s *ear, holds him almost like a lover.*

Scene Three

Fergus *and* **Ness**. *Bedroom. Night.* **Ness** *stroking* **Fergus**'s *hair, seducing him, rejecting him. A game they both play.*

Fergus
>I'm hoarse with saying it.
>He won't hear from anyone but you:
>If you want him saved,
>If you want him to be King

Tell him to grant pardon,
Let them return.

Ness

Your hoarseness will be worn to silence
Before she's back in Ulster.
She should burn for this:
I'd make her crawl for pardon.

Fergus

And Naoise had no part in it?

Ness

Only the part of man.
As you had part
In saying spare her.

Fergus

And say it still:
If they come back,
She must be pardoned too.
Let Conor find another bride,
Find one for him, let him have a son.
Give Naoise and his brothers
Enough to say they're not dishonoured.
Let Conor build his power,
Build it so his grip won't slacken
When you and I are dust.

Ness

Do you trust me?
Do we trust each other?
How do I know what you think
Or what you're planning for us?
How do you know what my mind is?

Fergus

Who'd know that?
You fooled me once,
I'm not so easy fooled again.
I know you see clear enough

To know they must come back.
Make Conor see it too.
He must agree a treaty:
It's the only choice for all of this to hold.

Ness

But it's a galling thought, this treaty:
Who's to say that they'll accept?
Who's to say they won't come back
And sow the seeds of vengeance?

Fergus

Every truce is galling.
And every seed of vengeance
Conor sowed.
They want peace and life in Ulster;
Once this treaty's real
They'll keep their word.

Ness

How do we know that?

Fergus

Did I keep mine when I came back?
Even in the face of all I saw around me,
Did I break the word I gave?
Naoise's bound by the same codes
And holds his honour just as high.

Ness

Every code he flouted when he left with her.

Fergus

And Deirdre had no part in it?

Ness

Only the part of woman.

Fergus

So we're equal.

A body knows no law
When it finds another.

Ness

If I persuade Conor,
Make him agree all this,
Will you go to Scotland –
Bring them back?
It's the only way they'll know
Our word is true.

Will you do it?
Will you do it for me?
Will you go?

Scene Four

Deirdre *and* **Naoise** *in Scotland.* **Deirdre** *working on*
a tapestry, which she later rips apart.

Deirdre

There's too much darkness here
And too much gloom,
The people are sour-hearted,
They nail all brightness down.
We should have gone to Scythia
Or Greece, to sun, gone south
Away from this midge-infested rain.

Naoise

Look at you,
You'd scorch in eastern gardens,
You'd wither up and die.

Deirdre

I'm wilting now for want of sun.
I'm parched for blue of sky.
I cannot stay on this besodden rock.
If I had swallow's wings I swear
I'd fly to where I'd breathe in heat.

Naoise

Then go, then try,

And see how far
Before you fall.

Deirdre

I'd sooner go than stay:
Look – is this what I was born for?
To weave and loom and loom and weave
And stitch and darn and sew.
Have I not eye to hunt
And hunter's hands –
This work is woman's woe.

If I were Queen in Ulster
I'd not be fixed to this –
I'd have slaves to do it.
How can you see me so reduced?
If you were a man
You'd take me back,
Face Conor down,
I know that he'd give in to me.

Naoise

And have us killed?
My uncle to give in!
It would be madness to go back,
Much as my heartstrings pull me.

Deirdre

It's madness to stay here –
And drives me to the arms of madness.

Naoise

I thought our love was world enough.

Deirdre

It is – enough and more.
You *are* my world,
But here the sky has shrunk,
The ground we walk grows smaller,
These walls edge closer every day.
Don't you see:
My heart is withering,

My eyes are smothered
By confinement and this drudgery.

Take me back to Ulster –
I'll inveigle Conor to forgive,
Our fame will pave a path for us.

Naoise

A path straight to the grave.

Deirdre

You sound more like a woman
Than a warrior.
Are you afraid of Conor?

Naoise

I fear no man or woman.
I fear no King.

Deirdre

Then why don't we return?

Naoise

I'd give up half my life to go –
But I'll not risk yours.
If you knew my love of Ulster
You'd not taunt me to go back;
Each day away from it burns me;
If you're too cold here
I'm on fire with want;
With want of all the places
That are here inside me but are gone.
With loneliness for all I've lost.

Deirdre

If I'm not fearful to return
What holds you back?

Naoise

I fear what came in sleep.

My brothers, too,
Saw the same omens
On the same night:

Two birds in flight
From Eamhain Macha
Landed here;
Two ancient eagles.
They carried in their beaks
Three drops of honey.
They spill the honey out –
One drop
To each of Usna's sons.

Deirdre
And none for me?

Naoise
And when they leave
They take three drops of blood.

Deirdre
What warrior would grudge
One drop of blood against a future?

Naoise
Would you sooner be a soldier
Than a woman?
Well?
And what about the battles?
I can see you now, moaning,
Gurning, nothing right:
Your sword too blunt, your shield
Too small, your clothes too tight –
Or maybe not too tight.
A boyish pout, you catch the leader's eye,
A wink, a flex of muscle, silent promise:
'Imagine this slim body in your bed.'
You'd be spared another minute's fighting,
Need be, you'd rouge your cheeks with blood,
See others dead that you might live.

Deirdre
And is that so inhuman?
Do *you* fight to live or kill?

Naoise

I fight for Ulster's honour.

Deirdre

Still you jabber 'Ulster'
Though in exile,
Still you speak of honour
Though in shame,
Would you not fight for *me*,
Make *me* your Kingdom,
Would you not shed your blood
To write my name?

Naoise

Is that, then, what you want?
Your name in blood?

Deirdre

And yours, too.
Our love immortal.

Naoise

Is mortal love
Not good enough?
What should I say?
'I'd give my life for you?'

Deirdre

Yes. Yes.

Naoise

The day we met
You talked of dying
As if love and death
Were one.
I said I'd sooner live,
And in our life together
Make a mortal love
That might be immortal.

Deirdre

And we will:
Your mortal child

Is seeded in my body.
I should be happy,
I *am* happy,
But I fear this stranger
In my womb
May be a force between us.

Naoise
That couldn't be:
Our child will forge
Our future and our joy.
Our life will trace a line
Across the hand of time.

Deirdre
Why do all men want
Themselves born over?
Is my body not enough?
Or must you see a Naoise mewing
At this breast
Before you know content?

Naoise
I'd be as happy
With another Deirdre.

Deirdre
I'd not:
I'd be as happy as we are.

Scene Five

Conor, **Fergus** *and* **Ness** *at Eamhain Macha.* **Conor** *seated,*
Ness *beside him, mainly silent, watchful, complicit.*

Conor
I've thought on it:
They must come back.
I've turned it all
A thousand times in mind,

And see the wisdom of your words;
I won't pretend there's not a sour taste
In their repeating, but I know their truth.
The Kingdom is divided and won't unite
Until they're home. That they're my nephews
Doesn't make the wrong they've done the less;
But they *are* my nephews and what Felim said
Is true – I've loved them almost as my own.
I know the danger I've dragged down
By what I've done; I was a blind man
Raging at the light. Now I see again
And see the harm my flailing blindness caused.
I'll do my best to mend what I have broke;
I'll build up what's tumbled down, pay
What can be paid, make good the worst.
I know this must be done if I'm to reign,
If Ulster will be healed.

Fergus
You talk of everything but Deirdre.
You talk of reason, though it was
The heart that led you here.
Think on it:
Could you bear the sight of Naoise
On this soil again?
Will your sour swallow
For the sake of peace
Come retching up your throat
If you see her
Flaunting her pardon in your face;
If you see her
Reach for Naoise's hands,
Or kiss his lips, in full knowledge
Of your watching eye.
Will you hold, then, to this
Level-headed pitch?

Conor
Those very thoughts
Have kept me sleepless.

Those same imagined sights
Have filled me up with gall.
I've fought so hard
Against my own imaginings
That the sight of them before me
Would be no worse.

Ness

They'll have to show respect,
Vow loyalty, accept their part.

He'll marry –
Then we'll have an heir;
And she can be forgot.

Conor

I want you to go to them,
Bring them back;
There's no one else whose word
They'll trust so sure as yours,
And no one in whose hands
I'd place that trust but you.

Tell them they've free pardon,
They can return with you.
I'll drain the draft of bitterness
Straight down,
I'll welcome them right here
To Eamhain Macha.
It's the only way for everyone to see
The past is shut behind us
And we make the future
From its bones.

Bring Felim with you as persuader
He worked his words on me.

Ness

And I have done my part.

Fergus

If they refuse this pardon
Where do I stand then?

Conor
> They'll not refuse
> When news of it's from you.

> Will you go?

Fergus
> Nothing would bring me greater joy
> Than to see this truce made real.

Conor
> Then go with word of joy to them
> And bring them home.

He embraces **Fergus**, *gives him the gold necklace* **Ness** *has been wearing.*

> As token of good faith
> Take this to Deirdre.
> She'll know it from the past
> And know the past is over.

Exit **Fergus** *and* **Ness**. *Enter* **Cathach**.

Conor
> Tell Leabharcham to come.
> Wait with me:
> I need to think what's to be done.

Scene Six

Scotland. **Deirdre** *and the sons of Usna asleep. A hunting horn sounds three times. The men spring awake.*

Ainle
> We're surrounded . . .

Naoise
> No. That sound is Ulster. The note is Fergus.

Ardan
> Two figures in the valley in the mist.

Deirdre *stirs awake.*

Enter **Fergus** *and* **Felim**. **Felim** *holds back somewhat, watching*
Deirdre.

Fergus
We come as messengers of hope.
Conor grants you pardon
And wants you home with us to Ulster.
Come with us to Eamhain Macha,
I'll be hostage to your safe return.
I place my honour here before you.

Naoise
Your word is bond; I'd never doubt it.
These are the words I've longed to hear,
Yet doubt sounds out a note as clear
As those you made to tell us of your coming.
How do we know that Conor's word is true?
Did he speak of Deirdre?
How do we know he doesn't set a bait
To draw us like night badgers to a trap?

Fergus
I've knuckled all his words with him,
And see a man who's struggling in his core,
I've watched and weighed his every measure:
His offer's true.

Felim
We'd not deceive you with false hope.
Conor knows the cost of peace in Ulster:
The cost is your return and his pride upheld.

Naoise
We're honour-bound to go.
He knows we can't refuse this hand he offers;
If we do we lose all face
And may never step on Ulster's strand again.

Deirdre
What did he say of me?

Fergus (*taking out gold necklace,* **Conor***'s early gift to* **Deirdre**)
He sent this gift for you;
He said when you received it
You would know
The past is over
And a new day come.

Deirdre
This was his wedding gift to me.

'The past is over
And a new day come.'

I fear his mind
And what his meaning is.

He's setting up some snare,
The glint of this is proof.
His words are clear.

To send me this:
We can't go back.

Fergus
His words are words of pardon,
The gold shows his respect;
Another might have footed it
Into a shapeless ball
Or flung it far to dent the memory.

Deirdre
Instead he keeps it
And sends it on again.
We can't return.

Fergus
You're safe.
You're in my charge,
He'd not dare
To harm any one of you
While you're with me.

We're straight to Eamhain Macha
When we land.

Nothing can happen;
Once he's greeted you
He's honour-bound
To keep his word.

Deirdre
He's greeted me with this.
He might as well have sent
A naked kiss
To place upon my body.

(*To* **Naoise**.)
We mustn't go.

Naoise
We have no choice.

Deirdre
'Three drops of blood.'

Naoise
You scorned that dream
And urged us back to Ulster.
He'd not send that
If he intended harm.
We'll leave with Fergus.

Deirdre (*to* **Felim**)
I don't know who you are,
If your words persuaded Conor,
Use them now to keep us here.

Felim
I wish I had the words to say what's right,
The sight to know what's true.
You cannot know my grief to see you grieved;
If I knew the land of Conor's mind
I'd tell you stay or go; and go myself or stay
And watch your happiness with joy.
I was silent when I should have spoken,
A life I should have loved was held in balance –
I turned my eyes away.

I have no store of wisdom and less right
To tell you what is best, to sway
Your judgement back to Ulster or stop here.
We came in hope of peace;
We offer what we hope is true.

Deirdre

Your words nest deep within me,
As if I heard all this before.
An echo from a past,
From some sad shore
Beyond my memory.

Naoise's said he longs for Ulster,
He's told me of its beauty.
I've only seen a patch of it,
I was a bird caged up:
I had no father, only Cathach,
No mother, only Leabharcham.
Do you think if I go back
I'd find them?

Felim

You have no need of them.
Your life lives here beside you.

Naoise

And will never leave.
The boat waits on us . . .

Deirdre

Maybe in Ulster
We'll know peace.
Say again
We'll not be parted.

Naoise

No need of words:
Your heart's flesh
Knows it true.

Deirdre

My heart's flesh

Mourns this moment;
But I can't undo
What's done or is to be.

Naoise

The boat waits on us.

Deirdre

Then we'll go.

Exit all.

Scene Seven

Cathach *and* **Leabharcham**.

Leabharcham

I'll not go until you tell me:
Let him kill me or let you.

What message does he send to Fergus?

Cathach

He told me tell no one.

Leabharcham

And that's why I'm afraid for her.

Am I no one?
I know I've counted little,
Counted less than youth or man,
But think of Deirdre
Who has been my daughter
And your own.

This message may lay out her fate.

Cathach

I'm to meet them on the strand,
Wecome them in Conor's name,
Say how pleased he is they're home,
Praise their courage in returning.

Then I bid Fergus,
By all the ties that bind him
Leave the others for Dún Borrach
For the gathering of clans;
Say that Conor would be there
But stays instead to welcome Naoise.

Leabharcham
He snares Fergus in a trap of honour;
Conor knows that every pledge he's taken
Binds Fergus to attend.

Cathach
When Fergus leaves them
I'm to say Conor has prepared their welcome
In the Red Branch Hall,
More fitting than Eamhain Macha.

Leabharcham
More fitting if he means them harm.

Go, and bring his message;
I know you'll do it anyway;
Fergus has no choice but go as he's bid.
But there's still a choice for Deirdre and for Naoise;
Tell them to turn back for Scotland
And from there to travel far as they can go.
Make sure they turn.
Do this if you care for anyone at all.

I'll wait at Eamhain Macha,
Prepare for her arrival
As he'd have me do;
But pray the bitter prayer
That I'll not see her,
There or anywhere in Ulster.

Exit both.

Scene Eight

The Sons of Usna, **Deirdre**, **Fergus**, **Felim** *land on Ulster's shore.* **Deirdre** *may be veiled.* **Cathach** *meets them.*

Naoise
I fear we are betrayed:
Only the eyes of Conor come to greet us –
Where's the rest of him?

Ardan
He'd never welcome us except at Eamhain Macha.

Cathach
Conor sends his heartfelt welcome back to Ulster.
He waits at Eamhain Macha to greet you all himself.
Fergus, this for you . . .

He hands a note to **Fergus**, *who reads it.*

Fergus
He bids me go to Dún Borrach
For the feasting of the clans.
I'm to go in place of Conor
Who waits on your return.
I have no choice:
I go or stand disgraced.
(*To* **Cathach**.)
What way is Conor's mind?
You see us here –
The one you helped to raise
Returned home.
What is he planning?

Cathach
I only know he told me come
To meet you here;
And told Leabharcham to go
At once to Eamhain
To greet Deirdre there.

Deirdre
What of Naoise and my brothers?

Naoise
Well, Cathach, what of us?
What kind of welcome is he laying out?
If you're your master's tongue and eyes
You must have knowledge of his mind.

Are there no signs for you to read?

Cathach *downcast, silent.*

Fergus
If you're welcomed at Eamhain Macha
All is well;
No guest is harmed inside those walls.
Be on your guard if he sends word
To meet him elsewhere
Or to rest the night in any other place.

Cathach
He sends word, too,
That the Red Branch Hall
Is where your welcome's made.
I was to tell you this with Fergus gone.

Ainle
Then we're betrayed.

Naoise
The Hall is sacred to us,
He'd not harm us there.

Fergus
I thought I read his feelings
And his mind;
Now standing here
A chill of doubt is colder than this wind.

Naoise
I know for honour's sake
You have no choice but go.

It leaves us bare:
With you beside us he'd not
Dare to change his word;
Now we journey on
Uncertain of a welcome
Or betrayal.

Felim

We brought you here.
The boat is in the bay;
You can turn back.

Naoise

I will not be turned from Ulster twice.
I'll not have him say
He offered pardon and we ran.

Deirdre

I would say no,
Turn back;
I should have said
I'd not return.

Too late;
We must go on.

Fergus

Felim, go from here, go fast,
Tell Finn and Roe, my bravest nephews
To join with Deirdre and the sons of Usna,
To rouse as many men as will gather round them
To be their watching hands
Since mine are tied.
Send quick to me with word if danger comes,
I'll raise a troop to down him if he breaks his bond.

Ainle

We should raise that army now.

Fergus

And give him cause for war?
He'd say you broke your word,

Came home to take the crown.
Enough for now you have protectors,
Men who gather round
To make you welcome home

Naoise
What Fergus says is true.
We must go on.

Fergus
The gods be with you.

Felim
And be with us all.
Deirdre,
You are home,
Closer to kin
Than you may ever know.
Don't let your courage fail you now.

Exit **Fergus** *and* **Felim**.

Cathach
I have told you all.
May I speak with Deirdre?

Deirdre *nods her head.*

Cathach
Leabharcham tells you to turn back.

Deirdre
We must go on.

Cathach
Ardan,
By all that you hold dear
And all that you remember,
Tell them to go back;
The boat is there
And all your lives within it.
Go on from Scotland,
Keep travelling towards the sun.

Ardan

The past is over:
We must go on.

Naoise

There's nothing more to say.
Cathach, your work is done:
Tell Conor we wait for him
And what he plans.

Cathach

Ardan,
Look at me:
Tell them to go back.

Ainle

We are all one mind
And will not retreat.

Deirdre

Tell Conor
We are one.

Exit all.

Act Five

Scene One

Deirdre *and the sons of Usna arrive in the Red Branch Hall.*
A meal is laid, a table set, but no one else is there.

Naoise
See, all is ready,
The table set;
The King sits here,
And Ness beside him;

Deirdre
This is where it ends,
The table laid
For death to have his fill.

Naoise
Where are we?
Yes, here,
The honour-length away.
All is as it should be,
Only no one here
To share it with us.

Deirdre
This is where it ends.

Ardan
Only no one here
To stand with us;
To share this bitter meal.

Ainle
No one here;
Betrayed, we stand together.

Deirdre
This is where it ends.

The men eat, begin to prepare their weapons, maybe braid their hair or make some other ritual preparations for a fight. They do so calmly, accepting what is to come. A knocking is heard.

Ainle
They're here.

Leabharcham*'s voice is heard calling* **Deirdre***'s name.*

Deirdre
No. It's not yet time.
Open the door:
That voice is echo of my own.

Enter **Leabharcham***. She and* **Deirdre** *embrace, hold each other,* **Leabharcham** *weeping, touching* **Deirdre***'s face, her hair;* **Deirdre** *composed, calm.*

Leabharcham
My sweet daughter,
O my half of life,
To see you here
Should fill my heart with joy –
And does.
But this must be as fleet
As swallow's day:

(*To all.*)
You are betrayed,
The siege is planned,
The troops are on their way.

(*To* **Deirdre**.)
Conor sends me with this word:
If you'll come back with me,
To him, Naoise and his brothers
Will be spared, and get safe passage
Out of Ulster.

Naoise
We will never leave.

Deirdre
I will never go.
He'd betray his word again,
Kill them when I'm gone.

Leabharcham (*to all*)
Then leave, go now, without a moment's pause;
The gods who cherish love will be your guide,

Naoise
We cannot leave again.
Now we're here
We're honour-bound to stay.
Deirdre stays here with us.

Deirdre
Go back to him,
Say I have grown withered –
The rains of Scotland
Soaked the best of me,
There's truth in it.

Say never again the Deirdre
That he knew.

Leabharcham
He'll not believe it:
He'll send some other to report.

If you'll not leave,
Then come back with me
And speak to him:
He's hungered for you every day,
His soul is hollow from the fast
And seeks to ease starvation
With great bloodied mouthfuls of revenge.

Let him see you:
Heal his eyes
And then his heart may heal.

Deirdre
He sent me this – (*Showing the necklace.*)

He thinks I'll be his bride.
Take it back to him,
And say I'd wrench my own heart
From my breast and send it to him
So he could gorge his injured pride,
But *I'll* not go.

Deirdre *tries to give the necklace to* **Leabharcham**.

Leabharcham
I'll not take it –
It would be like setting kindling
To a smoking fire.

The first sounds and the first flickering flames of siege are seen.

Deirdre
That fire is lit:
No act or word of mine will douse it.

The women embrace. Exit **Leabharcham**. **Ainle** *and* **Ardan**
mount to the battlements to watch the scene outside; **Deirdre** *and*
Naoise *sit down to play a board game – early Irish chess. The siege
gathers in.*

Deirdre (*to the brothers watching*)
What do you see?

Ardan
Fergus kept his word.
His nephews, Finn and Roe,
Have thrown a circle round
To shelter us.

Ainle
Legion of the Red Branch,
Standing with them:
Gone from Conor.

Naoise *and* **Deirdre** *play on. The siege intensifies.*

Deirdre
What do you see now?

Ardan

> A fire of battle on the snow.
> The lines advance, retreat
> Like twin seas that face each other's tide.

Ainle

> Each retreat leaves frothings on the shore:
> A scattering of limbs, the moaning dead,
> A hand that clutches at the chilly air.

Naoise *and* **Deirdre** *play on. A lull in the battle sound.*

Deirdre

> Has it finished? Who has won?

Ardan

> They rest.

Ainle

> The ravens come;
> Two hundred scald crows rise and fall again.

Naoise *and* **Deirdre** *play on.*

Deirdre

> What was the thing of greatest beauty
> In your life?

Naoise

> The sight of you that morning, naked.

Ardan

> That morning, too;
> We sat and watched the morning grow.

Ainle

> My brothers swimming
> In the river's light.

Deirdre

> The dream I dreamt of you
> And of us all.

Naoise *and* **Deirdre** *play on.*

Ardan
The battle starts again:
Roe is wounded.

Ainle
Roe is dead:
His men fall back.

Ardan
Conor comes forward,
The battle stops.

Ainle
Finn goes to him,
The ranks part for him.

Deirdre
He will betray us.

Ardan
They talk. Finn turns.

Ainle
He is bought and fights against us.

The brothers descend from the battlements to go out to fight. **Deirdre**
speaks as they begin to move.

Deirdre
Then you must go.

In silence, with a ritual of touch, **Ardan** *and* **Ainle** *say goodbye to*
Deirdre *and* **Naoise***, then exit to fight.* **Deirdre** *and* **Naoise**
play on; then **Naoise** *ascends the battlements to watch the scene of*
battle outside.

Deirdre
What do you see?

Naoise
My brothers like two dancers in the snow;
They hold the horde at bay −
Their swords are faster than the eye.

As fierce and fast as two young wolves
They move among the living and the dead.

The siege draws back, but gathers force again:
Conor at its head.

The snow is muffling life –
Clean limbs are falling;
The hacking axe is whirled
As joyful as the plaything of a boy.

Their men are scattered now:
I must go out to them.

Deirdre
Tell me, before you go,
Of Ulster's beauty.
I never saw it.

Naoise
It is not as beautiful as you:
Yet it's my life:
By day it is as green and fertile
As a tree fresh drenched by rain.
At night the skies are endless,
With stars cut out of all the glorious dead;
The moon now palest blue, now red, now yellow,
I swear it must be the loveliest sky
In all the world.
The journey down to Tara,
Some day you'll see it:

The way the land rolls back
And opens out,
The plains of whitest cattle,
Swift rivers full of trout,
The little rolling hills,
The forests full of deer,
The clear blue lakes
Which hold the world in perfect upside-down;
Each tree, each rock, each shore of waving sedge

So glassy true the lake might be the world
And world water – maybe is.

Deirdre

Don't go:
Love's power is the only force we have:
If we can raise it now
And make it like a flame
To scorch the fires that blaze around,
Then we burn beyond these walls of siege
And burn and burn and live;
And take your brothers with us
From this wounded snow.

Naoise

Love's power is not so great,
And I must go:
Live, that I may live if I should die:
Your eyes will look on day and see,
And it will be as if my eyes, too,
Are seeing light;
And these sweet ears will hear for me,
Will hear night fading into dawn,
The joyful throat of morning open wide,
Its song defiant, heard anew each sun,
And heard again by me, though I am gone.

They kiss, hold each other. Exit **Naoise** *to battle.*

Deirdre

How can I bear to hear the dawn without you?
If you die, I am dead, all but this life in me.

She ascends the battlements. Looks out.

He was hunting with two others;
　　　It was winter.
The deer was young and lithe.
　　　The snow
Was everywhere, great branches
　　　Silent in the white of day.

What do you see now?

They cornered him upon the crest of Manaun,
    His fawn cried in a hidden slope;
He was dappled with the light
    Of autumn appling.

He was trembling, with his hands
    Upon her throat.

A thread of blood runs round;
    The stitch unravels,
His head held back, the grip
    A tautened bow:
The thread is drawn again,
    The main knot severs –
His life pours hot and staining in the snow.

Deirdre *stands waiting for her fate, for* **Conor**. *He arrives with bloody hands.*

Conor (*showing his right hand, then his left*)
The red upon this hand is Naoise,
And this his brothers' blood.

Look – see their severed heads
Now raised aloft above the field of battle.

Deirdre
I look, I cannot see;
My eyes are blinded.

She begins to take off her clothes.

Take me, Conor;
This is the body you have waited for.
Its soul is fled.

Conor *advances upwards towards* **Deirdre**, *wiping his bloody hands on his clothes. Stands before her, touches her cheek tenderly, stares at her, then suddenly hits her hard across the face, knocks her down, rapes her.*

Scene Two

Fergus *stands in the ruins of battle, sets his course for Connaught and revenge.* **Felim** *standing with him.*

Fergus
  And so I am betrayed;
  The worm of fear that brooded in my gut
  Was bred in fertile ground,
  The muck and blooddirt of this Ulster Court.
  With Ness to stir and heat and watch
  That all the hatching came to being;
  And Conor, watching her,
  Learnt well the art of masks,
  The donning of a face to hide the face that is;
  And mummed an act of bitter,
  Thought-through peace,
  Revealing what I thought to be his thought,
  But hiding his true pulse
  So deep within him that I couldn't see.

  Eyes so hungry for the light,
  They looked past darkness,
  And thought the waving strands of night
  The tattered remnants of a bloodied flag
  Torn down, discarded
  For the sake of Ulster's peace.

  What choice, but raise a new flag now,
  Avenge these deaths and my unmanly fate;
  They sent me to be gelded and I went,
  A blinkered stallion to the pasture slope,
  Now time to kick the walls, and break,
  Now time to trail the fetter-rope
  Of my undoing in the dust to Connaught.

  There we'll gather strength,
  And there we'll plan
  The downfall of this house
  And all within.

Exit **Fergus** *and* **Felim**.

Scene Three

Ness *and* **Conor**. *Eamhain Macha. A sense of decay, things come undone. Both dishevelled.*

Ness

Fool, Fergus gone to rouse up Connaught:
You've written our undoing
In the bloodied snow.
I watched the soldiers' faces
When you killed the three;
They were masks of quiet hate.
And though you've gained a victory,
The very reins we hold have slipped
From us in all this mire.

You killed the men we needed,
All for her,
She's the one should die.

Conor

You told me what to do.

Ness

I told you to send Fergus,
To lure them back –
To containment, not to slaughter.
They'd have been our hostages,
Foundation for the future we'd have shaped.
But you were blinded by this lust for her
And you have killed yourself in killing them.
And you've killed me.

Conor

Deirdre lives.

Ness

Deirdre lives!

If I had thought it through,
We'd have let them settle,
Let a wheen of days go by,

The truce become well-bedded
In their minds before we moved.
And in the lull of time,
Deirdre would have slipped away,
No marks, no stains, no trace,
To point a finger, or to say
Her death was anything but sleep;
A sleep as sure and sad as life.

Instead, the Sons of Usna die
And Deirdre lives!
If that snow-blooded creature
Is alive at all.

Conor

Alive – and with new life within her.

Ness

And what will she bring out?
No son of yours
But Naoise's spawn
To grow up and destroy
Whatever's left by then.

Conor

The child is mine.
I know it.
Our son will live.
He'll see Ulster thrive
When Fergus is old dust.

Ness

The child is Naoise's
If it is at all;
There's nothing in her
Or she hides it well.

Has Cathach read
To see what's there?

Enter **Cathach**.

Cathach (*to* **Conor**)
The stars say he's your son.

Ness
The stars! The stars are not enough.
Was there not flesh to jumble in and find an answer?
There should be enough of it.

Cathach
I did ungut a life and look:
A young bull sacrificed to bring us peace.

Ness
What did that ungutted calf reveal?

Cathach
I couldn't tell:
The signs were mixed,
(*To* **Conor**.) The liver – you;
The heart said Naoise.

Ness
Then the child must die.
If not, he'll grow up to avenge all this.

Cathach
But which sign is true?
If the child is Conor's
And you kill him,
That's the end of it.
Alive, he is your life.

Ness
Only one can tell us that.
We'll find her and we'll know.

Exit all.

Scene Four

Deirdre *and* **Leabharcham**, **Deirdre** *holding her baby son.*

Deirdre
Our son is born
And I must go.

Our life renewed:
His mouth, his hands,
His heart and mine.
Naoise, but not Naoise.
How could I watch you grow
And not be him?
How could I see your eyes
Without his soul?
How could I hear his voice
From other lips?
How could I give you love
And not hate his absence,
And hate you?

(*To* **Leabharcham.**)
Take him far away:
Rear him as you reared me.
Let him know our story,
Let him know of Naoise and of Deirdre,
The story of the sons of Usna
And how we were betrayed.

(*To baby.*)
I leave you in the arms of Leabharcham,
Mother to me
And my guide to life.

Deirdre *hands the baby to* **Leabharcham**. *Moves to exit.*

Leabharcham
Where are you going?
Deirdre, the moon is dimmed by cloud,
The sky is hiding all its light
And all the pathways will be gone.

Deirdre
One pathway leads me home.

Exit **Deirdre** *to throw herself to her death from the battlements onto the rocks below. We may hear her death cry.* **Leabharcham** *holds* **Deirdre**'s *baby.*

Leabharcham
She stands on the battlements' edge,
Looks out and up,
Does not look back.
Now raises her arms;
The moon comes out;
She steps, she falls . . .

(*To baby.*)
Your eyes shall not see this
You must never know
The broken way she fell,
Her mind asunder on the rocks.
You must believe
She steps and flies,
Dips low to kiss the earth,
Then rises up to meet the three who come
Like birds of lightning and who make
Her name sound in the Heavens' chasm
With their beat of wing
And their wild call.

All four climb high
And still their flight
Swoop down again:
Then aim themselves
Like arrows at the sun.

I close my eyes against the light,
Then look again –

They're gone.

Scene Five

The feasting hall at Eamhain Macha where the play began.
Leabharcham *stands holding* **Deirdre***'s baby. Enter* **Conor,**
Cathach, Ness. Leabharcham *climbs up, away from them,*
going higher as the scene progresses.

Conor
Where is she?

Ness
Give me the child.

Cathach
Leabharcham, where's Deirdre?

Leabharcham
Deirdre's gone.
This child is Naoise's;
You'll not have him.
He'll grow up to avenge it all.

Ness
How do we know he's Naoise's
But to see him?
Give him here, into my arms . . .

Conor
If he's mine, he'll live;
As you will live
And be a nurse to Ulster.

Leabharcham
His eyes belie the lie
Your mouth has made.
His eyes are Naoise's
With a spark of Deirdre's.
I know that light – and know too well
The vengeful shade of your intention.

Cathach
Can our eyes not judge?
If you give the infant here;

Let *me* look, on my soul
The child will live,
Whatever the knowledge that I learn.

Leabharcham
Give you this child?
To feed and nurture into future day?
When every moonlight
Found you far away.
As distant as my heart is now from you.

As distant as this child for ever be.

Do you think me fool?
Give you their son –
To see him straight in Conor's arms
And strangled there?

Cathach
Give me the child;
I swear no harm shall come to him.

Conor
I swear it, too.
How could I harm
This child we made?

Leabharcham
And Ness . . .
Do you swear it?

Ness
Yes, I do.

Leabharcham
As you swore it safe for Naoise to return?
Liars! The gods tear out your bitter tongues.
Better this life be sacrificed by me,
These learning lungs be stilled by hands that love
Than choked to silence by a hateful claw.

And if my eyes misread these eyes
And this be yours;
More power to my hands this work to do.

Leabharcham *kills the baby.* **Conor** *is overcome with grief, believing the baby to be his.*

Enter **Fergus** *and* **Felim***; Felim carrying the body of* **Deirdre**.

Fergus
  We come too late
  With all the strength of Connaught.

Felim
  Too late to save her
  As I should have.

Leabharcham
  You come too late for Ulster:
  This is her child and Naoise's
  Who lies dead.

Cathach
  Now all is done.
  All I foresaw,
  And in the telling
  May have brought to being.

Ness
  Done.
  Let me look at her:
  Deirdre, what's left of you?
  The mould of head
  Within its nest of hair
  Broke open,
  Your frogspawn brain
  All blubbed and jellied –
  So your mind at rest!
  My heart should soar.
  This sight so long now
  Longed for that it seems
  A picture from behind my eyes
  Has flung itself to life
  And then to death:
  The hated blood
  Pulsed from you,

Voice, eyes, every vicious
Scheming sense stubbed out:
But a lifetime's span too late.
Had you been pitched,
A screeching infant from this battlement,
Our story would be different now.

Fergus

Have you no mercy still?

Ness

Mercy! Hopeless fraying
Of determined minds:
The wine of will so watered down
It's scarcely worth the drinking
Or the spitting out.

Looks at body, remembers, gloats.

People will say 'Deirdre'
When they mean a crawling,
Crippled thing, a torn bag-mask
For a face, a rag of hair,
Four twisted, flapping limbs,
Two teeth in a jagged smile.

I say again:
Look what your mercy's brought . . .

Did you contrive it, Fergus,
Nurture mercy in his breast
Knowing it would be our ruin?

I feel no grief for what lies here
And expect no mercy.

All is done.

Conor

'No grief, no mercy';
Nothing left.

(*To* **Ness**.)
Why isn't it you who lies here
Dead and silenced;

Deirdre alive and at my side; our son,
Whose mingled seed and history
Would bring greatness,
Heir to Ulster's throne,
His head held high
To place this crown upon.

It was you we should have killed
That Samhain night.
That was her call to me
Before she came to life.
How did I not hear?
All silent now.
All is done.

Fergus
Done.
This peace brought down
Not by the innocent who lie here,
Not by fate alone
Or what the stars or bloodied entrails
Lit or hid from sight . . .

We gather here again, as we did
That Samhain,
When it seemed that peace was sealed
And we drank to future day.
So well she might have cried, Deirdre,
From her mother's womb –
Cried for what she knew would come
From such cracked and sullied pledges.

Ness, you brought me back
To guard your son
And keep your grip on power;
Too late to guard him against you
And from himself,
The self you made him.

A twisted balance might have held
But for the tilt of fate that came

In the shape that lies before us broken now:
All Deirdre's store, and ours incarnate here.
The marching road from Connaught
Bringing conquest,
This Kingdom gone . . .

Felim

Our life a fallen deer.
This one I should have held
So tightly in my arms
And wrapped out evil from her,
Wrapped out all this
Before her life began.
Too late. Now all is done.

Red Branch Soldiers *lead* **Conor** *and* **Ness** *away.*

Leabharcham

Done.
Within my arms a sleepless infant,
The waking dreams of life all shuttered now;
The shades of love adrift in famished gardens,
The mouldered kisses broken in the clay.
Give single cry, all Ulster, to this passing,
Let muffled heart-bells toll the grieving way;
The horsemen near,
Hear fall their shadowed hoof-beat;
Quench out all light –
Let darkness rule the day.

The **Bulls of Day** *and* **Night** *re-enter, blood-stained, battered.
They face each other, embrace, kiss; the* **Bull of Night** *kills the*
Bull of Day. *They lie down together.*